Ten-step *Bible* Study Method

An Abbreviated Version

Johann Lai

Ten-step Bible Study Method : An Abbreviated Version

Author: JOHANN LAI
Translator: RICHARD SAM
Consultant: DR. ROY B. ZUCK
Reviser's: KAREN LEE, CALEB LAI
Editor: JOSEPH YIU
Designer and Layout Maker: ESTHER YONG

Published, produced and solely distributed by
Sacred Logos Resource Center (SAGOS)
846 Stewart Drive, Sunnyvale, CA 94085, U.S.A.
Tel: 408-773-8891
Fax: 408-228-6490
Email: info@sagos.org
Website: www.sagos.org
Printer: Ocean Printing Co. Ltd.
July 2012, First Printing
Product number: B024
ISBN: 978-1-4675-1242-8

CONTENTS

Preface v

Part One : Presentation of the "Ten-step Bible Study Method" 1

I. OBSERVATION SECTION 5
Step # 1: Get the Facts (FACTS) | *7*
Step # 2: Sort out Relationships (RELATIONSHIPS) | *11*
Step # 3: Analyze the Structure (STRUCTURE) | *16*

II. INTERPRETATION SECTION 18
Step # 4: Ask Questions (QUESTIONS) | *21*
Step # 5: Provide Answers (ANSWERS) | *23*
Step # 6: Summarize the Meanings (SUMMARY) | *36*
Step # 7: Find the Controlling Theme (THEME) | *37*

III. APPLICATION SECTION 40
Step # 8: Write down the Principle (PRINCIPLE) | *40*
Step # 9: List Specifics (SPECIFICS) | *43*
Step #10: Put into Action (ACTION) | *45*

IV. CONCLUSION 46

Part Two : An Illustration Using the "Ten-step Bible Study
Method": Acts1:8 51

Epilogue 73

Appendix: Basic References for Bible Study 75

A Brief Introduction of Sacred Logos Resource Center 78

Book Recommendations 80

Introduction of Author 83

PREFACE

My book *Practical Hermeneutics* (Chinese) was published in 1994. Over the last decade, I have had opportunities to give lectures in various places on how to use Practical Hermeneutics to study the Bible, teach "Hermeneutics" courses in Chinese seminaries, and conduct Bible study camps on the "Ten-step Bible Study Method." Through these various channels of teaching, I have seen how the "Ten-step Bible Study Method" can provide a workable Bible study approach for Chinese churches. Therefore, between January and June of 2008 I revised and expanded the content of the book to make it more complete. The title of the book was changed to *Ten-step Bible Study Method*, and it was published in July of the same year.

In the course of conducting seminars, many friends who were dedicated to Bible study expressed their appreciation that the material in the book is exhaustive and detailed. However, they suggested that if a simple list of the steps involved in the ten-step Bible study method could be provided so that its essence could be grasped without the time-consuming reading of the entire text, then it would be more helpful.

It is in response to this need that this booklet, *Ten-step Bible Study Method: An Abbreviated Version*, was written. It provides the basics of the operational procedures of the method. It is easy to follow so that first-timers may learn to use it quickly. After the main text, I present an illustrative example using Acts 1:8 as the Scripture passage so that readers may see how the method is applied.

I would like to emphasize that the Abbreviated Version is only for beginners, Referring back to the original *Ten-step Bible Study Method* would be needed for any explanation or clarification, as it provides the foundation of the theory of the method.

Johann Lai
May 15, 2012

Part One

Presentation of the "Ten-step Bible Study Method"

Method is a tool, it promotes efficiency in performance.
It also serves as a road sign, pointing to the goal and direction.
When functioning as a servant, it provides the greatest help it can ever give;
but when put in commanding position, it creates chaos and confusion.

—Selected

The Bible has always been acknowledged as the most translated and best-selling book in the world. However, this fact alone may lead to a misunderstanding of its value merely as a commercial commodity. In fact, thousands upon thousands of people who have bought the Bible do not read it at all, but they treat it as a decoration, an amulet, or a fixed asset. In many families the Bible has become a frozen asset, a forgotten treasure.

Is it "bitter" to study the Bible? Of course there are times when studying the Bible is hard. When the reader is unwilling to or is forced to study, or when the reader encounters a passage without comprehending it even after searching long and hard, it is bitter indeed. Is it "joyful" to study the Bible? Of course there are also times when studying the Bible is joyful. In Psalm 119:24, the psalmist said, "Your statutes are my delight..." Whether the Bible study experience is bitter or joyful depends on the attitude of the reader.

Furthermore, as Oletta Wald stated in the beginning of her book *The Joy of Discovery in Bible Study*, "While all Christians agree that the Bible should be studied, many do not find joy in their study. They know very little about the Bible and feel that it is difficult to understand. To them it is a strange book, seemingly too hard or too dull, and they have little inclination to read or study it. This is a tragedy, because Bible study can be a most rewarding, challenging, and exciting study. It can really be fun!" [Oletta Wald, *The Joy of Discovery in Bible Study* (Minneapolis: Augsburg, 1975), p. 7.] The key to whether or not studying the Bible becomes a dreaded task is in finding the right "way." When the correct method is employed, Bible study can bring endless joy.

The correct pathway to interpret the Bible is to follow a tested and true method, which includes a systematic procedure, principles, and steps. Establishing an effective system and method can provide a way that can be followed, a method that can be utilized. It can save time and increase efficiency. It also allows one to find answers to specific questions. A successful Bible interpreter must first establish an effective interpretation system with proper steps.

While the importance of a "method" is an undeniable fact, the interpreter must also recognize its role in the process. A "method" is just a tool, a channel to get from point A to point B. Its purpose is to serve man, not to set limitations. Furthermore the method must be practiced frequently to a high level of proficiency, in coordination with a seeking mind, the use of precise tools and the ability to integrate. Then it will become like a second nature.

The "Ten-step Bible Study Method" combines the principles from inductive Bible study and the principles of traditional hermeneutics. It employs the structure of inductive Bible study—observation, interpretation, and application—while injecting established and time-tested hermeneutical principles into the interpretation section. In addition, a model using "application based on theological principles" is also incorporated into the application section.

TEN-STEP BIBLE STUDY METHOD

Observation
1. Facts
2. Relationships
3. Structure

Interpretation
4. Questions
5. Answers
6. Summary
7. Theme

Application
8. Principle
9. Specifics
10. Action

Indeed, recent biblical scholars have discovered that there is no such thing as a purely inductive Bible study method, and they have to some extent incorporated into the structure of their inductive methods some established hermeneutical principles to complement the shortcomings in the interpretation section. Such back-and-forth employment of inductive and deductive methods of biblical interpretation are heavily emphasized in this book. In this way the simple steps of the inductive method are preserved while a rigorous and practical theological foundation is provided by the method. The two approaches are complementary to each other, giving the learner a clear way to study the Bible while also gaining an in-depth appreciation of the message of the Scriptures.

I. OBSERVATION SECTION

There is a basic difference between an explorer and a tourist.
The tourist travels quickly,
stopping only to observe
the highly noticeable or publicized points of interest.
The explorer, on the other hand,
takes his time to search out all he can find.

—MICHAEL P. GREEN

In the observation section, important facts and relationships in the Scriptures are noted, and the overall structure is divided into paragraphs. During this stage the Scripture must be examined, and any questions should be reserved for the interpretation stage. This first stage is focused on gathering information in order to be ready for the interpretation stage.

Observation is the step in which the eyes of the soul are used to find facts, differentiate behaviors, and observe happenings. It attempts to answer a question: "What have I seen?"

A. The Principles of Observation

1. Observation is the first step in Bible study. The more time one spends on observing, the less time will be needed to be spent on interpretation.

2. Observation must be thorough and careful. A skillful observer must be interested in the examination of details like a detective with inexhaust-

ible curiosity. He will not rest until he has found the truth, or the clue to it.

3. While observing the Scripture passage, awareness of the direction and ranking of the details is necessary. Missing the meaning of the whole by paying too much attention to the details should be avoided.

4. Observation must be objective and true to the text. Wearing a pair of colored glasses will only allow the reader to see what he wants to see. Instead, openmindedness in research will reveal what is contained in the text.

5. Observation must be addressed from different angles. Different perspectives need to be examined through different layers and fields in order to dig out all the facts.

6. Frequent practice makes observation perfect. In the beginning, it may be stiff or difficult to grasp the facts because of a lack of familiarity; but with time and practice using the right method, proficiency can be developed in the process.

B. The Procedures of Observation

1. Purchase a notebook and record your observations in it. Writing your observations is an effective part of the observation process, making it more interesting.

2. Carefully read the Scriptural text once, treating the passage as if you are reading it for the first time. Do not take it for granted that since you have read the passage before, you may muddle through it this time.

3. Use different methods to read the Bible, or listen to Bible audiotapes or CDs. Reading and listening bring about different senses of feeling and understanding. Reading the Scripture out loud also brings one to a new

state of mind as compare to reading it silently. Using Bible versions that have the text arranged in different forms may yield surprising rewards.

4. Read different Bible translation versions side by side, such as the NIV, NASB, KJV, or RSV, and contrast the differences in translations. New insights may be discovered.

5. Observe the details of the Scriptures in depth. There are two important aspects of observation: first, the observation of the facts, and second, the relationships between different facts. It is easier to observe the facts. Just distinguish its nature and write down the results. However, it is more difficult to observe relationships. Sometimes the complicated interrelationships of the facts may cause confusion between observation and interpretation.

6. Observation must be purposeful and systematic. Searching without purpose could be a waste of effort. If the reader does not know what to look for, then he will not find anything.

Step # 1: Get the Facts

To examine the facts is to find out the details in the passage regarding people, happenings, and things, and then label them with prepared labels. In order to facilitate readers to learn how to go about doing this task, the following table lists 17 items that frequently appear in Scripture passages, and provides brief descriptions of each.

OBSERVATION ITEMS	MEANING
1. Genre	The genre or literary style is the most basic of observation items. The Scripture has different genres such as narrative, exposition, poetry and song, wisdom literature, parable, type, prophecy, etc.

OBSERVATION ITEMS	MEANING
2. Character	The basic constituents of narratives. There are major characters (lead) and minor characters (support).
3. Time	There are two aspects in the observation of time. One aspect is to find out the timing of the incident within the timeline of human history, and the other is to trace what happened before and after the incident and how they are related.
4. Place	The location where the incident happened.
5. Situation	Usually the introduction to a new setting in a narrative, providing its background and circumstances. It appears in conjunction with the change of time and place, and can occur in a public or private gathering.
6. Comment	An explanation added by Scriptural authors during the course of a narrative so that the reader may have a better understanding of its meaning.
7. Emphasis	A special treatment by the author through grammatical arrangement of phrases or repetitive terms to add emphasis. Such arrangements allow certain parts to stand out in order to get the reader's attention.
8. Quotation	Appears when the Scriptural author inserts verses, idioms, passages, or even entire stories written by others into his work. There are two kinds of quotations: direct and indirect. • Direct quotation—quotes the exact words without any changes or omissions from the original into the text. • Indirect quotation—modifies, deletes, or summarizes the original verses, yet preserves the original message.

OBSERVATION ITEMS	MEANING
9. Question	A rhetorical device in literature when the author tries to get attention as well as to elicit thinking by using a question. • A real question is a question that anticipates an answer. The Bible has many such examples. • A rhetorical question is an assumptive question without anticipating an answer; it is a literary application that serves as an affirmative statement.
10. Command	Statements that must be obeyed. Usually they are important counsels that appear in the form of imperatives.
11. Promise	Statements devised to encourage or urge the reader in the blessings of the Lord. There are two kinds: conditional promise and unconditional promise. • Conditional promises require certain action from the claimer before the blessing. • Unconditional promises do not require the recipient to take any action first.
12. Warning	A statement that predicts potential dangers. They are commands put in a negative form.
13. Illustration	A truth, concept, or idea explained using everyday life experiences or historical incidents.
14. Theological Concept	Terms and phrases that are loaded with theological meanings, which in themselves carry significant weight.
15. Key Word	Words or phrases that have significant influence on the meaning of the passage.

OBSERVATION ITEMS	MEANING
16. Figurative Language	The use of a different wording to express an idea or to describe a situation. From the perspective of the author, there is a common feature between the two.
17. Difficult Term	Terms appearing in the passage that are hard to understand, which include proper nouns, geographic names, historical terms, or rarely used terms. The student should list them and consult Bible dictionaries to find their meanings.

The 17 items listed in the table above can help the reader recognize them in the process of observation. However, these are just basic suggestions, and interpreters may make their own labels as needed.

During the observation stage, the flow of the Scripture should be followed and these characteristics should be identified verse by verse, and labels should be applied to appropriate terms or phrases. However, one should not seek to find as many labels as possible in the passage. Of course not all 17 labels will be found in every passage. Just put on labels as they come up and write down the results of the search, in order to get ready for the interpretation stage.

Exercise for Step #1

Read the NIV version of Acts 1:8 three times.

"But you will receive power when the Holy Spirit comes on you; and you will be My witnesses in Jerusalem, and in all Judea and Samaria, and to the ends of the earth."

From the list of 17 items on the preceding pages, apply labels to the basic facts of the verse. Do not be concerned about missing something, only identify the facts you can recognize and say what they are.

Please write down your observations and compare with this booklet's illustration on Acts 1:8, which is shown on pages 52-53.

Step # 2: Sort out Relationships

To "sort out relationships" is to find out how the verse describes and arranges the facts and find their interconnecting relationships.

A total of 22 items belong to the relationship category. They are listed in the following table for ease of reference.

OBSERVATION ITEMS	MEANING
18. Context	The important key to unlock the message of the text. It includes the preceding context and the following context. It provides the logical and literary link to the author's flow of thought, and helps the reader grasp the dominant theme of the verse.
19. Climax	The central focus of the entire passage, whether it is in the main passage or in an episode.
20. Summary Statement	A concise statement of the nature or purpose of a passage.
21. Contrast	The association of two things, terms, or ideas that are opposite to each another to achieve a desired effect.
22. Comparison	The association of two things, terms, or ideas that are of the same category to achieve a desired effect.

OBSERVATION ITEMS	MEANING
23. Repetition	The repeated occurrence of identical or synonymous terms, phrases, or ideas in the verse. Their appearance represents the author's emphasis or the passage's main points.
24. Atmosphere	The effect of the passage on the reader, based on the tone, the speed, the development of the plot, and the movement of circumstances. Different descriptions of atmosphere include calm, tense, dangerous, joyful, suspenseful, and miserable.
25. Grammatical Structure	The grammatical relationship among words, phrases, and sentences. In general, words are classified as follows: (1) nouns and pronouns with the following elements: subject, direct object, indirect object, gender, number; (2) verbs, with the following elements : its tense (past, present, future and perfect), voice (active and passive), and mood (indicative, subjunctive, and imperative); (3) other classes such as adjectives, adverbs, conjunctions or prepositions, etc. In addition, the change in usage and the appearance of abnormal applications should be highlighted.
26. Significant Connective	The grammatical devices that connect one clause, sentence, or paragraph to another. Frequently used connectives include and, or, but, if, because, for, as, therefore, so, in order that, etc.
27. Digression	A statement inserted by the author that is not part of the main thrust of the passage.
28. Progression of Ideas	A technique by which the author arranges a number of terms or phrases in sequence from low to high, or from small to big, to elicit climax and attention.

OBSERVATION ITEMS	MEANING
29. Comparing Translations	Unless the reader has a firm grasp of the original languages, he must depend on various translations. By comparing different translations, the reader can interpret a verse, a phrase, or a term from different angles, so that he can understand the probable meaning of the Scripture, and also perceive potential issues from the different translations.
30. Qualitative Relationship	The relationship the author wants to portray, comparing or contrasting the quality or nature of the things discussed.
31. Quantitative Relationship	The comparison or contrast between two things in terms of capacity, size, weight, or number.
32. Spatial Relationship	The distance or other related concerns between two places, cities, or countries.
33. Chronological Relationship	Compares incidents in the times, dates, and even ages of their occurrence, and the significance they carry in understanding the text.
34. Sequential Relationship	The portrayal of things or ideas in terms of their order and sequence of appearance.
35. Relational Relationship	The relationship among people in terms of biological, spiritual, or emotional relations.
36. Cyclical Relationship	The back-and-forth interaction that passed between two or more points, places, and persons.

OBSERVATION ITEMS	MEANING
37. Authority Relationship	The relative levels of authority between persons or offices, and who must be accountable to whom.
38. Causal Relationship	A certain thing or incident may be a cause or a result of another thing or incident. A causal relationship demands that the cause happens before the result. In other words, there must be a time sequence between the two. Further, there must be an entailment relationship between the two. Therefore, if A and B have a causal relationship, then A entails B, or A brings out B. In other words, B coming into being is based on A's existence.
39. Omission	Something that under normal circumstances should have been included, but was absent. It could have been intentionally omitted to bring out a point.

These items of observation are like labels that must be placed appropriately according to the flow of the Scripture passage. Any insight should be written in the notebook for use later in the interpretation stage.

To memorize these 39 items of observation may seem difficult. However, it is not necessary to memorize these items right away. With continual practice, observational skills can be developed as time goes by.

The process of labeling is to collect information, using one's eyes to discover various items. All the questions raised can be addressed in the fourth step "Ask Questions."

Exercise for Step # 2

Read the assigned Scripture using 3 to 4 different translation versions:

NIV
"But you will receive power when the Holy Spirit comes on you; and you will be My witnesses in Jerusalem, and in all Judea and Samaria, and to the ends of the earth"

NASB
"But you will receive power when the Holy Spirit has come upon you; and you shall be My witnesses both in Jerusalem, and in all Judea and Samaria, and even to the remotest part of the earth."

KJV
"But ye shall receive power, after that the Holy Ghost is come upon you: and ye shall be witnesses unto me both in Jerusalem, and in all Judaea, and in Samaria, and unto the uttermost part of the earth."

AB
"But you shall receive power (ability, efficiency, and might) when the Holy Spirit has come upon you, and you shall be My witnesses in Jerusalem and all Judea and Samaria and to the ends (the very bounds) of the earth."

Place labels on the basic relationships of the verse. This is the same as Step # 1. Do not worry about missing anything. Just identify the relationship labels you observe and write them down.

Write down your observations. Compare them with the illustration on Acts 1:8 on pages 53-55.

Step # 3: Analyze the Structure

Based on the relationships discussed above, the Scripture verse can be tentatively divided into paragraphs. Structural analysis is to determine the message the author is seeking to convey through the relationship between words and sentences of the Scripture. This must be done by looking at the big picture, or the overall flow in the verse.

Two kinds of literary structure may be observed. One is "obvious structure," such as the ordering of words and phrases, the use of grammar, and important connectives. In the Bible study process this part is observation. The other is the "hidden structure," which is more implicit and thus not readily recognized. This will become apparent only after the step of interpretation is followed. In this step only the "obvious structure" will be noted.

1. Identify two kinds of structure

a. Obvious structure can be discerned from the emphasis of the verse, the use of connectives, etc., and belongs to the observation section.

b. Hidden structure will become apparent only after one interprets the verse, and so this belongs to the interpretation section.

2. To find the structure of an exposition passage

a. Identify the boundary of a paragraph by noting the emphasis of the Scripture and important connectives, etc.

b. Determine the progress of the thought of the passage.

c. Pay attention to the context and the progression of ideas.

d. Find the thematic sentence of the Scripture, and then attach related concepts under the thematic sentence.

e. Divide the passage into 2 to 4 smaller paragraphs according to the flow of the Scripture.

3. To find the structure of a narrative passage

The structure of a narrative passage can be regarded as movements in a symphony, or as scenes in a play.

    a. Identify the boundary of a paragraph: the appearance of different scenes based on changes in characters, things, or events. If all three change, then it must be the beginning of a new incident. If two out of three change, it may be a new scene.

    b. Note the plot of an incident. A plot is "the principle or intention that holds the incidents together." It is the essential element required for the understanding of incidents, episodes, and progress of actions of a narrative.

    c. Once the plot and scenes of the narrative passage are found, analyze its structure for further subdivision.

    d. Divide the narrative into 2 to 4 smaller paragraphs according to the flow of the passage.

Exercise for Step # 3

Acts 1:8 is a sentence spoken by Jesus; thus it can be treated as an exposition. Write down the tentative structure of Acts 1:8 and compare with the illustration provided in this booklet on pages 55-56.

II. INTERPRETATION SECTION

Let it be said at the outset—and repeated throughout,
that the aim of good interpretation is not uniqueness;
one is not trying to discover what no one else has ever seen before...
The aim of good interpretation is simple:
to get at the "plain meaning of the text."

—GORDON FEE and DOUGLAS STUART
(*How to Read the Bible for All Its Worth*, p.16)

After going through the various steps of observation, the interpreter has already answered a basic question: "What have I seen?" In addition, he has also collected a lot of raw material about the Scripture. The many steps of interpretation attempt to answer another question: "What is the meaning of what I see?" Their purpose is to process the raw materials gathered from observation in order to produce useful "products." Overall the process of observation is simpler, whereas the process of interpretation is complex and multifaceted.

The purpose of interpretation is to find the original meaning of the author, by asking questions about the content of the Scripture, and then answering each of the questions. After the meanings of each of the paragraphs are summarized, the main theme of the passage is identified, which is the central message the author intended to convey through this Scripture.

The steps of interpretation are built on the steps of observation. The following table expresses the relationship between observation and interpretation.

OBSERVATION	INTERPRETATION
1. Investigates the "what" of the Scripture	1. Investigates the "why" of the Scripture
2. Uses the eyes to answer a question, "what have I seen?"	2. Seeks to answer the question, "What is its meaning?"
3. Emphasizes facts and their interrelationship	3. Emphasizes skills to interpret, comments on or judges the observed facts
4. Is simple and direct	4. Is complex and multifaceted

There are four steps in the interpretation process.

A. Interpretation Principles

1. Unless the Scripture itself gives clear indications, each passage or each term should have only one interpretation under normal circumstances. While there is only one interpretation of any given passage, there can be many applications.

2. The interpreter should seek to discover the meaning and the message of the passage, and not be prejudicial and force theological concepts onto it.

3. Straightforward and simple interpretations are often more reliable than complicated interpretations.

4. To interpret a difficult and obscure passage, it must be compared with simple and direct Scripture. In other words, certain passages that are generally considered controversial cannot be used as the sole basis of a person's faith and behavior.

5. Differentiate descriptive from prescriptive Scriptures, noting their differences.

DESCRIPTIVE	PRESCRIPTIVE
a. Narrative style	a. Expository style
b. Describe the progress and development of an incident	b. Expound on the application of a truth
c. An example or warning to believers	c. A principle or command to believers

6. Understand the difference between meaning and implication and note which implication(s) is(are) conscientiously placed there by the author, and which one(s) is(are) not.

7. Pay attention to the unity of thought in context, and use the preceding and following Scriptures to help interpret the meaning of the passage.

8. Recognize that every passage of Scripture has a message conveyed by the author at a given time to a specific group of readers. Therefore the relevant cultural and historical backgrounds must be noted.

9. The understanding of the grammatical structures and relationships among the words and phrases is fundamental to finding the meaning of a passage.

10. Speculate on the possible meanings of each word, and discover how they are used in the text.

11. Through comparison with similar passages or Scriptures with the same theme, find out the dominant teaching of the biblical revelation.

12. Differentiate between figurative and literal speeches. When encountering figurative speech, proper interpretation principles must be followed to determine its meaning.

13. Follow the logic and deduction used in literary communication to determine the original meaning of the author.

14. Take note of the specific literary genre of each passage, such as narrative, exposition, Hebrew poetry, wisdom literature, parables, prophecy, type, or revelation literature. Different genres come with different characteristics and emphases, which can help in determining the meaning of the passage.

15. For controversial or difficult passages, come to your own conclusion first, compare it with commentaries, and then select the most reasonable interpretation.

B. Interpretation Procedures

Step # 4: Ask Questions

In this process the interpreter must continually raise different questions about the content of the Scripture in order to help explore the deeper meaning of the Scripture. In general, there are three types of questions: questions of definition, questions of logic, and questions of implication.

1. Questions of definition or explanation. These questions ask for the meaning and explanation of a word or phrase. For example, "What is the meaning of this sentence?" or "What is the author trying to say with the use of this term or phrase?"

There are at least three types of words or phrases in the Scripture that need to be defined or explained: key terms and phrases, theologically loaded terms, and obscure and difficult terms and phrases.

2. Questions of logic or relationship. These questions are used to determine why certain statements were made and to see the relationship between them. For example, "Why did the author put it this way?" "What is the role of this word in this sentence?" "What is the connection between this sentence and the preceding sentence?"

3. Questions of implication. These questions seek to ascertain the significance of the meaning of the Scripture. For example, "What is the significance of this verse to the overall meaning of the passage?"

The purpose of this question-and-answer section is to determine the meaning of important terms, and the development of the thought of the passage, in order to seek to discern what the author wanted to convey. In the process of asking questions, it would be best to write down all the questions for future reference.

Exercise for Step # 4

Write down 30 questions related to Acts 1:8 based on facts and relationships you observe. When asking questions, do not be concerned if the question is weird or if you think it may not have an answer. Afterwards examine your questions and eliminate the questions that appear less relevant, reducing the number of questions from 30 to 20, and after each question note which type it belongs to: whether questions of definition/explanation, logic/relationship, or implication. Compare your work with the illustration in this booklet on pages 56-60.

The Ten Major Principles in Biblical Interpretation

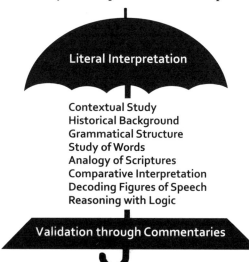

Literal Interpretation

Contextual Study
Historical Background
Grammatical Structure
Study of Words
Analogy of Scriptures
Comparative Interpretation
Decoding Figures of Speech
Reasoning with Logic

Validation through Commentaries

Step # 5 : Provide Answers

When all the questions are raised, each question must be addressed and answered according to the truth. To do that, ten time-tested hermeneutical principles can help us.

1. Find the point of the question and focus on it. Remember the purpose is to try to understand the meaning of the Scripture through answering questions.

2. Apply some time-tested principles developed by scholars over the ages to answer questions. These principles can be summarized into 9 categories: literal interpretation, contextual study, historical background, grammatical structure, study of words, analogy of Scriptures, comparative interpretation, decoding figures of speech, and reasoning with logic.
The first principle, literal interpretation, is the umbrella principle that embraces all the other principles. (see the picture on p. 22)

3. Each of the 8 different interpretive principles under this umbrella principle has its particular function.

4. These interpretation principles should be applied collectively in a complementary manner. With practice, one can become acquainted with them and proficient in applying them, thus becoming skillful at the task of interpreting the Scripture.

5. The principles stated above are applicable to Scriptures of any literary style, and thus are called general hermeneutical principles.

6. When all the questions are answered, the interpreter may compare his work with commentaries that record opinions from other scholars or experts, and summarize an interpretation most suitable for the Scripture as his own conclusion.

7. Finally, acknowledging ignorance is a safety outlet when all avenues

to interpretation are exhausted. However, this last resort should not be used frequently.

Principle # 1   Literal Interpretation

1. Definition

In a nutshell the literal method of interpretation employs the most natural, most normal, and most general usage of language to interpret the Scripture. It seeks to explain the meaning of the text, as intended by its author, according to the normal usage of its language (the meaning expressed by the words), basic grammatical rules (combination of grammatical structures), and historical facts (actual circumstance of the incident).

2. Procedure

a. The literal method has three emphases:
   i. Grammatical structure—exact meaning of words, their functions, and the relationships among words.
   ii. Historical background—cultural environment, time of writing, and all other circumstantial factors that may affect the author in writing the Scripture.
   iii. Nature of the writing—genre analysis, literary style, organization of materials, figures of speech, etc., and how they affect the meaning of the text.

b. The literal method interprets the Scripture through historical background, grammar, and normal usage of the language. It is based on objective facts rather than subjective imagination or speculation.
c. It recognizes that the authority lies in the Scripture and therefore allows the Scripture to speak for itself, rather than allowing the interpreter to read his own thoughts and ideas into the text.
d. The method utilizes objective criteria by which interpretation can be evaluated.
e. The method includes figurative and typological interpretations.

Therefore a distinction can be made between two kinds of literal interpretation, the general literal and the figurative literal. Both are legitimate within the scope of the literal method.

Principle # 2   Contextual Study

1. Definition

Contextual study seeks to interpret the Scripture following the relationships between sentences and words based on thoughts that run through the passage.

The principle of context is the most important one among all interpretation principles. In fact many other interpretation principles follow its lead and are subordinate to it.

2. Procedure

a. For convenience, study the immediate context consisting of the 2 or 3 paragraphs that immediately precede or follow the passage.

b. Note words or phrases that repeat themselves. These words are hints that help in interpreting the Scripture.

c. For Scriptures that seem to lack direct contextual relationships, look up the author's purpose of writing the book.

d. After studying the context of the Scripture, try to fill in a "Contextual Study Table" to elaborate their interconnecting relationship.

Principle # 3   Historical Background

1. Definition

Every Scriptural passage is written by its author at a certain time, for specific readers, and to deliver a specific message. Therefore the interpreter must speculate on the meaning of the Scripture through his understanding of the prevailing history and cultural background.

2. Procedure

a. Investigate the historical background of a book or passage from the Bible.

b. Speculate on the motivation and purpose of the author from the passage itself.

c. List the other important background material from the passage or the book:
- Customs and habits
- Moral concepts
- Social class structure
- Racial prejudices
- Education status
- Religious factions
- Weather and seasons
- Geographical factors

Principle # 4   Grammatical Structure

1. Definition

Grammatical structure refers to the way the author utilizes the building blocks of words, phrases, and sentences to construct a message to convey meaning. Before studying its grammatical structure, one must be able to differentiate between different kinds of literary units. This principle is concerned with the grammar of the original language and English. The literary units are divided into two major categories: nouns and verbs.

Differentiating the grammatical types of each word or phrase is only the first step in the study of grammatical structure. Words, phrases, and sentences are merely tools in the hands of the author to be utilized in conveying a message. Literary relationships between the words and phrases (or syntax) must be understood in order to bring out the meaning of the Scripture.

Syntax is the set of rules that govern the formation of sentences with words and phrases. When an author conveys a message through literature, he will usually follow general linguistic rules.

2. Procedure

Categories of words

Noun Types
1. **Noun**—A name for a certain thing, person, place, or concept.
2. **Pronoun**—A word used to replace a noun.
3. **Adjective**—A word that describes a noun or a pronoun. It points out the degree, quantity, or attributes of the noun or pronoun it qualifies.
4. **Preposition**—A short phrase placed before a noun or a pronoun. It shows the relationship between two or more clauses in a sentence.
5. **Conjunction**—A word that connects words, sentences, or paragraphs.
6. **Article**—In English grammatical structure, there are indefinite articles (a, an) and definite articles (the).

Verb Types
1. **Verb**—A verb is a description of the action or identity of a noun or a pronoun. To study a verb, its tense must be noted. The tense of a verb indicates the time during which the action described by the verb takes place. Tenses can be classified into perpetual (present), past, future, and perfect.
2. **Adverb**—The chief function of an adverb is to qualify a verb.

Verb Types
3. **Participle**—A participle is a verb used as an adjective or an adverb. Participles are usually attached to the principal verbs in the Scripture.

Interrelationships among words and phrases

TERM	MEANING	EXAMPLE
1. Agent	Through whom does it come?	In Romans 5:1 the fact that "we have peace with God" is "through our Lord Jesus Christ." Therefore Jesus Christ is the agent through whom we have peace with God.
2. Basis	What is its occurrence based on?	In Ephesians 1:7, "the forgiveness of sins" is based on "the riches of God's grace."
3. Content	What does it include? What does it consist?	In Romans 5:3-5, "suffering produces perseverance, etc." are the content of the phrase "we know."
4. Contrast	What is its other face?	In Romans 5:7-8, "Very rarely will anyone die for a righteous man, though for a good man someone might possibly dare to die…While we were still sinners, Christ died for us." Dying for a righteous man and for a good man are contrasts to Christ's dying for sinners.
5. Description	What is its nature? What characteristics does it have?	In Colossians 1:15, "He is the image of the invisible God" is a description of an earlier phrase, the "Son he loved."

TERM	MEANING	EXAMPLE
6. Explanation	What is its meaning?	In Ephesians 6:3, "you may enjoy long life on the earth" is an explanation of "go well with you."
7. Manner	How did it happen?	Romans 5:8 says, "But God demonstrates his own love for us in this: While we were still sinners, Christ died for us." How does God demonstrate His love for us? By Christ's dying for sinners.
8. Means	Through what means does it come? By what did it occur?	In Romans 5:1, "since we have been justified through faith" indicates that faith must be the means to justification.
9. Object	Who (or what) is the recipient?	Romans 5:8 says that "While we were still sinners, Christ died for us." We are the object of Christ's death.
10. Place	Where does it happen? (geographical)	In Ephesians 1:1, "To the saints in Ephesus" indicates that Ephesus is the location of the recipients of the letter.
11. Purpose	What is the motivation?	In Ephesians 1:6, "To the praise of his glorious grace" is the purpose of the activities in verse 5.
12. Reason	Why is the principle correct? Why did it happen?	Romans 5:3 says, "but we also rejoice in our sufferings." Why would we rejoice in suffering? "Because we know that suffering produces perseverance."

TERM	MEANING	EXAMPLE
13. Repetition	Which phrase does it repeat?	In Romans 13:5, "Therefore, it is necessary to submit" repeats verse 1.
14. Result	What is derived from it? What is its consequence?	In Ephesians 6:3, "that you may enjoy long life on the earth" is a result of "honoring your father and mother."
15. Source	Where did it come from? What is its source?	In 1 John 4:7, "for love comes from God," shows that God is the source of love.
16. Sphere	Where did it happen (nongeographical)?	In Ephesians 6:1, "in the Lord" is the sphere of "obey."
17. Time	When did it happen?	Romans 5:8 says that "while we were still sinners, Christ died for us." When did Christ die for us? It was when we were still sinners.

Principle # 5   Study of Words

1. Definition

The study of all the possible meanings expressed by individual words, and the selection of the specific meaning it must be given in the Scripture.

2. Procedure

    a. Because words develop into new meanings through history, it is always helpful to trace their historical development.

    b. Word study should consider the context.

c. Word study must be prioritized based on its theological content.

d. In word study one must not give an inappropriate meaning to a given word in a given context.

e. A word can have a double meaning when allowed by the Scripture.

Principle # 6 Analogy of Scriptures

1. Definition

The gathering of several similar doctrines or incidents together in order to be compared, in an attempt to understand the Scripture from different perspectives.

2. Procedure

a. The interpretation of each Scriptural passage must be consistent with the overall doctrines of the Bible.

b. Identify which two or more Scriptural passages are parallel passages of the same theme.

c. When a passage mentions one aspect of a certain doctrine, one should then see if other Scriptures also mention different aspects, and whether it is consistent with the overall teaching of the Bible.

d. The analogy of Scripture is based on the principle of progressive revelation of God.

e. Unclear or obscure passages must be interpreted in light of the clear ones.

f. From the perspective of progressive revelation, the New Testament is the "fruit," and the Old Testament is its "root." Therefore New Testament Scriptures should carry a heavier weight.

Principle # 7   Comparative Interpretation

1. Definition

Comparative interpretation is a principle under the analogy of the Scriptures. In accord with the unity of the Scriptures, it compares two or more similar or parallel passages of the same incident, so that the meaning of an individual Scripture passage can be seen from different perspectives.

2. Procedure

a. Comparing Scriptures can enrich the meaning of individual Scriptures and make them stand out, highlighting areas that are less noticed, turning simple narrative into something special.

b. Comparing two or more writings of the same incident or similar incidents can complement each of the passages and clarify the meaning of the incident or discourse, and answer some potential questions raised.

c. Before comparing, individual Scriptures must be studied first, and then put together for comparison.

d. Comparing Scriptures is not an exercise to "fill in the blanks"; it is not an attempt to fill in the missing information in the passages.

e. If two passages appear to be in conflict with each other, the interpreter must pay attention to the following two important points:
   i. It does not imply that the Bible is not self-consistent.
   ii. One should attempt to resolve the conflict between these two Scriptural passages.

Principle # 8   Decoding Figures of Speech

Communication among human beings is accomplished through language or literature. In the process of communicating, not only is straightforward narrative employed, but also much figurative language is also used. Thus the correct hermeneutic principles should be used to interpret figurative or symbolic languages.

1. Definition

Figurative language is a variation of literary expression that differs from straightforward description. The meaning of one concept is brought out through the use of comparison, substitution, omission, or addition.

2. Procedure

a. The use of figurative language is not to obscure the meaning of the Scripture, but to make it clearer and livelier.
b. Literal interpretation should be employed wherever applicable.
c. Note carefully the context of the passage and determine whether the text should be interpreted literally or figuratively.
d. In interpreting symbolic texts in figurative language, its true meaning must be found before applying it to the concept or thing to which it is being compared.
e. Pay attention to the cultural and historical backgrounds of a figurative language.

Different kinds of Figurative Languages

Comparison	Substitution	Omission	Addition
Simile	Metonymy	Ellipsis	Pleonasm
Metaphor	Synecdoche	Aposiopesis	Hendiadys
—	—	Zeugma	Repetition

Contradiction or Contrast	Overstatement or Understatement	Imitation
Irony	Hyperbole	Personification
Litotes or Meiosis	Euphemism	Apostrophe
Antithesis	—	—
Paronomasia	—	—
Oxymoron	—	—

Principle # 9   Reasoning with Logic

1. Definition

Reasoning with logic is finding the meaning of Scripture through the normal thought processes of literary communication.

2. Procedure

a. Biblical interpretation must be based on common sense.
b. A truth or a doctrine cannot be developed based on the idea that it is not mentioned in the Bible.
c. Differentiate between definition and description.
d. Do not make conclusions based on overgeneralizations.
e. Beware of the mixing of terms, which violates the argument of "application with the same assumption" in logic.
f. Logical reasoning and the exercise of imagination are not mutually contradictory in biblical interpretation.

Principle # 10   Validation through Commentaries

1. Definition

The principle of validation through commentaries requires that after the interpreter has arrived at a tentative conclusion, he is to compare and evaluate it with the views of other scholars and select the interpretation closest to the original meaning of the Scripture as the final conclusion.

2. Procedure

a. Do not be afraid of using commentaries.
b. Do not begin a study by going first to commentaries.
c. Commentaries are not "books from heaven" and free from errors.
d. The criteria for choosing a commentary must be its writing philosophy and publication purpose.
e. A good commentary will certainly point out the difficult issues with the Scripture passage.

Exercise for Step # 5 (please compare with the illustration on Acts 1:8 on pages 60-69)

Please answer the 20 questions raised in Step # 4 in accord with the 9 basic principles of interpretation. The 9 basic principles are: Literal interpretation, Contextual study, Historical background, Grammatical structure, Study of words, Analogy of Scriptures, Comparative interpretation, Decoding figures of speech, and Reasoning with logic. After you have answered each question, please attach to it the principle you used in answering the question.

After you have tentatively answered all the questions, look up any difficult terms or phrases that require comparison with commentaries, so that you are assured that the answers provided are not mistakes or deviations from the correct answers. Several useful commentaries on Acts are these:

Barrett, C. K. *A Critical and Exegetical Commentary on the Acts of the Apostles*. 2 Volumes. Edinburgh: T & T Clark, 1994.

Bruse, F. F. *The Book of the Acts*. Revised edition. Grand Rapids: Eerdman, 1988.

Longenecker, Richard N. *Acts*. The Expositor's Bible Commentary. Vol. 9. Edited by Frank E. Gaebelein. Grand Rapids: Zondervan, 1981.

Marshall, I. H. *The Acts of the Apostle*s. Tyndale New Testament Commentaries 5. Grand Rapids: Eerdman 1980.

Step # 6: Summarize the Meanings

1. Integration

Integrate and organize the results from Step # 5, "Provide Answers," so that the answers may be linked together to form an integrated meaning. Summation implies that the meaning of the Scripture can be explained in one or two sentences. There are two steps to this process:

First, collect and organize the results from the step "Provide Answers." Answer each question with one or two sentences. For certain difficult terms or questions that cannot be readily answered, consult a dictionary or encyclopedia to gather related material.

Second, find the Scripture's structure and tentative outline. If it is an exposition, follow the thought of the author and how he developed the controlling theme, using paragraphs and his progressive concepts. If the Scripture is a narrative, then identify the plot of the narrated incidents, so that different parts of the Scripture are properly placed in the overall structure.

 a. Organize and integrate the answers to the questions and find the core meaning of each verse or paragraph.

 b. Summarize the dominant thought of each small section.

 c. Organize the Scriptural purposes brought forth from different questions.

 d. Integrate the overall meaning of each small section.

 e. Find the controlling thought and main point expressed by the author in the Scripture.

2. Rewriting the Scripture

    a. Rewriting the Scripture means rewriting the meaning of the Scripture in your own words.

    b. The rewriting of the Scripture must be based on correct interpretations of the Scripture.

    c. Rewriting the Scripture is not retranslating the Scripture.

Step # 7: Find the Controlling Theme

Once the meaning of each small section is found, sort out the controlling theme of the Scripture. The controlling theme must be a complete sentence that summarizes the meaning of the entire passage. It must be a theological statement, not a historical description.

1. To find the controlling theme of the Scripture, one must understand the author's purpose for writing the Scripture, under what circumstance, and for what reason.

2. The controlling theme is the core of the Scriptural thought, the subject matter that permeates the words of the text, the "tree-trunk" meaning of the passage.

3. In a narrative the controlling theme of the Scripture is related to the plot of the incident. Through the description of the actions in the narrative, the author seeks to determine dominant purpose of the passage.

4. In an exposition the main theme of the Scripture is closely related to its topic sentence. If this topic sentence is found, then the rest of the Scripture can be developed and elaborated around this sentence.

    a. Understand the author's central purpose of writing this Scripture and how it relates to the main theme of the entire book.

    b. Find the subject matter that connects the sentences together, which is closely related to the topic sentence.

    c. Express the controlling theme of the Scripture in a single sentence.

The two steps "Summarize the Meanings" (including Rewriting the Scripture) and "Find the Controlling Theme" are the two final steps (steps 6 and 7) of the interpretation section of the Ten-step Bible Study Method. Their purpose is to look at the big picture and summarize the important thoughts of the Scripture. By organizing and integrating them, seek to determine its core purpose, which is the "tree-trunk" meaning of the Scripture.

Exercise for Steps # 6 and 7

Summarize the meaning of Acts 1:8 and find its controlling theme. Look first at the important theological thoughts of the verse and then write a controlling theme sentence. Compare your work with the illustration on Acts 1:8 on page 69.

"Theological Principle Application" Model

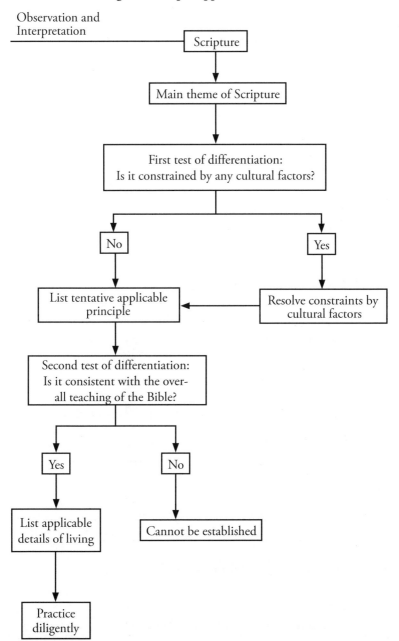

Observation and
Interpretation

Scripture

Main theme of Scripture

First test of differentiation:
Is it constrained by any cultural factors?

No

Yes

List tentative applicable
principle

Resolve constraints by
cultural factors

Second test of differentiation:
Is it consistent with the overall teaching of the Bible?

Yes

No

List applicable
details of living

Cannot be established

Practice
diligently

III. APPLICATION SECTION

Apply yourself to the whole text,
and apply the whole text to yourself.

—J. A. Bengel

Application means putting into practice the message and spiritual lessons of the Scripture in the life of the Bible interpreter.

Step # 8: Write down the Principle

Convert the topics of the small sections into a theological principle that transcends time and space (for New Testament epistles, sometimes the controlling theme of Step # 7 can become the principle in Step # 8), and with further processing, it can be turned into a spiritual lesson.

1. **The principle is a bridge between interpretation and application.**

Decide the meaning of the Scripture to the author's original readers	Write out the principle	Respond with a certain action
Interpretation (meaning)		Application (significance)

2. **The principle can appear in the following forms:**

a. It is an assertion or a positive explanation.

b. It is a clear and thorough proclamation, using a single word or a concise sentence to express an important thought.

c. It is a truth that is always effective.

d. It is a rule set up as a basis for everyday living and behavior.

3. The principle must be based on the overall theology of the Bible.

The theology mentioned here is biblical theology and not human thinking. The principle must transcend time and space, have everlasting value, and be consistent with the unchanging plan and truth of God.

4. Method and Procedure

The application of theological principles (see the flowchart on page 39) is to screen the theme of the Scripture through two differentiating tests, so that on the one hand it is liberated from limitations because of cultural differences, and on the other is consistent with overall biblical teachings.

a. Take the main theme obtained from interpreting the passage, and check it against the first requirement: "Is it constrained by any cultural factors?" If the theme is not affected by cultural differences, move to the next test. If, however, the theme fails to pass the first test, then the restrictions presented by the theme because of cultural factors must be resolved first.

b. After passing the first test, draft the tentative applicable principle.

c. Take the tentative principle and check it against the second test, and see if it is consistent with the overall teaching of the Bible. If inconsistencies are found, then adjust and correct the theme until the inconsistencies are removed. When the theme is consistent with the overall biblical teaching, it can become a theological principle suitable for application.

d. Apply the theological principle to practical needs by listing specific recommendations about living and practical actions.

One must find the "trunk" of the applicable Scripture before application can be practiced. The controlling theme is the trunk of the Scripture in the interpretation section. Once the trunk is found, the controlling theme can be bridged over to the application principle.

Bridging begins with the controlling theme in the interpretation section and consists of writing out the theological principle of the Scripture using the "Theological Principle Application" model.

    a. Convert the controlling theme into a spiritual lesson that transcends time and space.

    b. With the following method and procedure, determine the applicability of this spiritual principle:

        i. Check the controlling theme against the first test: Is the controlling theme constrained by the prevailing culture?

        ii. Write down a tentative spiritual principle (theological principle).

        iii. Check this spiritual principle against the second test: Is this principle consistent with the overall biblical teaching?

        iv. Modernize this spiritual principle and turn it into a spiritual lesson suitable for today's believers.

5. Cultural gap and application principles

    a. Note whether the passage or teaching contains truths related to a moral aspect or to God's will.

    b. Note whether the passage or teaching is restricted by the prevailing culture or habits.

    c. Note whether the passage or teaching contains theological principles or is just an illustration used to interpret a principle.

    d. Note whether or not the passage or teaching is focused on a certain improper practice that was prevalent during that time. The author might have stated it strongly to enhance the effect of the teaching rather than trying to express a general principle of God's will.

e. Note whether or not the passage or teaching is suitable for only a certain era, and was replaced later by other teachings.

Resolving cultural and historical differences is a very important link in the process of application bridging. Some cannot wait to apply the Scripture and treat it like flat land when it is actually a deep canyon, walking over it in wide strides, and ending up falling off a cliff. It is unfortunate that many interpreters think that they have already grasped the proper application of biblical messages, not knowing that they are just running in circles, as their conclusions are not built on the authority of the Bible.

Applying the model and flowchart of the "Theological Principle Application" will ascertain that the application principles so distilled have gone through thorough screening, and are not randomly applied.

Application must be specific. Broad-based and generalized application is equivalent to no application, as it tends to miss the mark, and also makes it difficult for one to follow through the truth.

Exercise for Step # 8

First, apply the two differentiating tests discussed above to the controlling theme of Acts 1:8, and then write down its theological principle that transcends time and space. (Please note: The application principle must be applicable in all places and at all times.) Compare your work with the illustration on Acts 1:8 on page 69-71.

Step # 9: List Specifics

1. Definition

List some practical details that may be applied in everyday life based on the spiritual lessons learned. (Note: The principle is general in nature, but details are specific; the principle is applicable in any era but details pertain only to a particular situation.)

43

2. Principles

Use the 5 letters of the acronym SMART as the 5 characteristics of application details:

S – Specific	Specific and applicable actions.
M – Measurable	The listed actions may be measured against certain standards.
A – Achievable	The listed actions are not unattainable, but for most people they are achievable given sufficient effort.
R – Relevant	The listed actions are practical and relevant, not wispy and hard to grasp.
T – Timing-related	The listed actions must be completed within a certain time-frame.

3. Procedure

a. Apply toward God, others, and self.
b. Apply in areas of knowledge, attitude, and action.
c. Actions may be in a group or by an individual.
d. Individual actions may include a spiritual aspect, an interpersonal aspect, a work aspect, or a social participation aspect.

Exercise for Step # 9

List specific actions based on the theological principle learned from Acts 1:8, so that you may put into practice the mission commanded by this Scriptural verse. (Note: The listed actions must be as detailed as possible, such as listing time, people, place, and specific actions, so that no ambiguity is left for guessing.) Compare your work with the illustration on Acts 1:8 on pages 71-72.

Step # 10: Put into Action

1. Actions must be immediate.

2. Remind yourself frequently.
    a. Write down your actions together with the Scriptural verse on a card or in a notebook, or even stick it on the mirror you face every morning.
    b. Habitually self-examine, evaluate, adjust, and pray to the Lord to give you strength to carry out what you have decided.
    c. Memorize the verses that contain the deeds to be acted out, and this will achieve the same effect as reminding yourself.

3. Ask a spiritual partner to help remind you.

Exercise for Step # 10

Put into motion the specific action plan derived from studying Acts 1:8. Before taking action, pray about these decisions, or ask one or two good friends to act with you, or ask your friend to pray for you so that you may fulfill your committed actions. Compare your work with the illustration on Acts 1:8 on page 72.

IV. CONCLUSION

To be proficient in a method or a skill, long-term training or professional coaching is necessary. Furthermore, in order to grasp the key to the method, putting the theory learned into practice is also necessary.

To follow through in learning, pay attention to three elements: development of interest, perseverance, and good planning.

A. Development of Interest

The success of many entrepreneurs came from their passionate interest in their chosen field of endeavor.

1. Practicality generates Interest

One of the reasons some believers find Bible study uninteresting is that they perceive that studying the Bible has little relevance to everyday living. However, this is a serious misconception. Biblical truth has a high degree of utility (see III. APPLICATION SECTION) as it contains many life-changing testimonies and messages.

2. Suitable method brings forth Interest

Many academic disciplines are difficult and inscrutable. If a pathway cannot be followed or if a method to study it cannot be employed, it will result in a lack of interest. However, if someone knowledgeable in the discipline can provide useful hints, it can become interesting to the students.

The goal of this book is to provide such guidance to the reader through the illustrated pathway and method, so that the reader may follow through, make steady progress, expand his interest in Bible study, and discover a new world of understanding.

B. Perseverance

"Rome was not built in a day!" Likewise, progress comes only through perseverance.

Someone said, "Fifty percent of success in life comes from 'Luck', and the other fifty from 'Discipline.'" The truth is that the second half is very important. Without discipline, you would not know how to manage your "luck".

C. Good Planning

A well-planned Bible study schedule can be very effective, but studying the Bible without planning will not last.

1. Set time
The human being is an animal of habits. If one is not determined to read the Bible daily at a given time and persevere, all plans are vain and will naturally perish. The best time to study the Bible is, of course, the morning. By gaining strength from the Word of God at the beginning of every day, it allows the day's activities to be built on a firm foundation. If Bible reading cannot be done in the morning, it is also fine to do it in the evening.

2. Humble beginning
Begin with short Scriptural books such as the Letters to the Philippians, James, or Philemon in the New Testament, or the books of Ruth, Jonah, or Haggai from the Old Testament. Study carefully with the method suggested by this book and practice often, then technique and proficiency will eventually be gained.

3. Record progress
Prepare a Bible study progress chart and record the actual progress daily as a reminder.

4. Write down insights

In addition, cultivate the habit of underlining Scripture or writing down insights gained from Bible study. This will help better understand the Scripture during the study, and it will also help to keep a record for future references.

As the saying goes, "A journey of a thousand miles begins with a step forward." There are numerous opportunities in life. Everybody has to take the initiative to grasp them and make an effort to use them. So stop stalling and act now!

The Altar of Biblical Interpretation

Knowledge	Attitude	Action

APPLICATION

Reasoning with Logic	Validation through Commentaries	Acknowledging Ignorance	Note the Genre
Study of Words	Analogy of Scriptures	Comparative Interpretation	Decoding Figures of Speech
Literal Interpretation	Contextual Study	Historical Background	Grammatical Structure

INTERPRETATION

Relational Relationship	Quantitative Relationship	Qualitative Relationship	Sequential Relationship	Spatial Relationship
Omission	Causal Relationship	Cyclical Relationship	Authority Relationship	Chronological Relationship
Atmosphere	Digression	Grammatical Structure	Progression of Ideas	Significant Connective
Contrast	Climax	Summary Statement	Repetition	Difficult Term	Comparing Translations
Illustration	Key Word	Theological Concept	Figurative Language	Context	Comparison
Emphasis	Command	Promise	Warning	Quotation	Question
Genre	Character	Time	Place	Situation	Comment

OBSERVATION

Bible: God's Book	Bible: Man's Book

Part Two

An Illustration Using the "Ten-step Bible Study Method": Acts 1:8

NIV

"But you will receive power when the Holy Spirit comes on you; and you will be My witnesses in Jerusalem, and in all Judea and Samaria, and to the ends of the earth."

NASB

"But you will receive power when the Holy Spirit has come upon you; and you shall be My witnesses both in Jerusalem, and in all Judea, and Samaria, and even to the remotest part of the earth."

KJV

"But ye shall receive power, after that the Holy Ghost is come upon you: and ye shall be witnesses unto me both in Jerusalem, and in all Judea, and in Samaria, and unto the uttermost part of the earth."

Step # 1: Get the Facts

This step consists of finding out the details in the Scripture regarding people, things, happenings, and basic facts, and then labeling their meanings with prepared labels.

To begin, read the NIV text three times.

NIV text:

"But you will receive power when the Holy Spirit comes on you; and you will be My witnesses in Jerusalem, and in all Judea and Samaria, and to the ends of the earth."

Now put labels on the basic facts found in this verse, using labels from pages 7-10 of this booklet. Do not worry that you may miss anything. Just identify these facts and say their meanings.

The observed results include:

1. **Genre**: This is an exposition within a narrative passage
2. **Characters**: Holy Spirit, the disciples (you), Jesus (I)
3. **Place**: Jerusalem
4. **Verbs**: will receive, comes on, will be
5. **Verb tenses**: all three verbs are in the future tense (compare translations)
6. **"Holy Spirit"**: a theological concept
7. **"Holy Spirit comes on"**: a difficult term
8. **"Comes on"**: an activity
9. **"Will receive power"**: a promise
10. **"Will"**: an emphasis
11. **"Power"**: a theological or difficult term
12. **"And"**: a conjunction
13. **"And you will be My witnesses"**: a command
14. **"The ends of the earth"**: a difficult term

Step #2: Sort out Relationships

This observational step is to sort out the interlocking relationships among the people, things, and happenings described in the Scripture, find any differences in interpretation by comparing translation versions, and finally indicate these relationships using the labeling method.

Putting labels (pages 11-14) on basic relationships in the Scripture is like the first step. Do not worry about missing anything so long as you write down all the recognizable relationships. The relationships include:

1. **"But"** is a conjunction that connects this verse to verses 6 and 7. It is a disjunctive relationship. It shows the relationship between the preceding verses and the text that follows it.

2. **Preceding context**: the disciples asked about the timing of the restoration of the kingdom of Israel.

3. **The meaning of Jesus' answer is**: the timing of the restoration is not something for the disciples to know. Then He said this verse to His disciples.

4. **Following context**: Jesus was taken up to heaven. Therefore this verse (1:8) is the last sentence uttered by Jesus that was recorded in the Bible.

5. **"The Holy Spirit comes on you (disciples)"**: the relationship between the "Holy Spirit" and "disciples" is that of "comer" and "receiver."

6. **"You will receive power when the Holy Spirit comes on you"**: a promise.

7. **"Will"** is an emphatic term. However, on comparing translation versions, the sense of "will" is not very strong.

8. **"Power"**: a theological or difficult term.

9. **"And"**: a conjunction. In the NIV version there are altogether 3 appearances among the 4 places mentioned.

10. **"Be My witnesses"** is a command, a command that appeared after a promise. (sequential relationship)

11. **"In Jerusalem, and in all Judea and Samaria, and to the ends of the earth"**: these 4 places are from near to far geographically. (progression of ideas)

12. **"The Holy Spirit comes on you"** and **"you will receive power"**: sequential relationship.

13. **"Be My witnesses"**: be Jesus' witness, witnessing on matters related to Jesus.

14. Both NIV and NASB use the terms "be My witnesses." (comparing translations)

15. **"Will receive power"** and **"be My witnesses"**: sequential relationship or causal relationship. The three verbs used in this sentence have dual causal relationships: "The Holy Spirit comes on" (cause) brings out "will receive power" (effect); "will receive power" (effect becomes the next cause) brings out "be My witnesses" (effect).

Step # 3: Analyze the Structure

There are two types of genre prevalent in biblical writing: narrative and exposition. The structure of a narrative is more hidden and is not necessarily discernable in the observation steps. If this is the case, we can wait and deal with it in the interpretation section.

Acts 1:8 is a sentence spoken by Jesus, and can be treated as an exposition by itself. Its structure can be expressed with these three short verbal phrases:
1. The Holy Spirit (will) come
2. Will receive power
3. Be My witnesses

Upon comparing three English translation versions, we found that all three of them placed "will receive power" ahead of "the Holy Spirit comes"; this is a normal usage of English grammar. However, logically "the Holy Spirit comes" should occur before "will receive power."

It is clear that these three verbs (come, receive, be) can have dual sequential or causal relationships. The cause "the Holy Spirit comes" brings about the effect "will receive power", and then "will receive power" becomes the cause of the next verbal phrase, "be My witnesses," as its effect.

Why is it so important to try to find the structure in the beginning? If a rough outline of the entire passage is revealed, then it will greatly help to speed up the progress of the following steps. As mentioned before, if the structure is not readily found, then wait for the interpretation section and do not try to force anything.

Step # 4: Ask Questions

Initial questions

In the beginning, ask as many questions as needed about anything that is not understood. Include the type of question behind each one as a reference to help in the study.

1. The Scripture begins with the word "but." How is it related to the question the disciples asked in the previous context? (question of relationship)

2. Why is it that Jesus did not directly answer the disciples' question, but rather brought forth the teaching of this verse? (question of logic)

3. What is Jesus' intended purpose in saying this sentence to His disciples? (question of explanation)

4. Who is the Holy Spirit? What are His characteristics? (question of definition)

5. What is the relationship between the Holy Spirit, God the Father, and Jesus? (question of relationship)

6. What is the meaning of the phrase "the Holy Spirit comes on you"? (question of definition)

7. Judging from the tense of the verb "come," when will the Holy Spirit come? (question of logic)

8. How will the Holy Spirit come? (question of explanation)

9. What is the phenomenon when the Holy Spirit comes? (question of definition)

10. What is the significance of the coming of the Holy Spirit to the disciples at that time? (question of logic)

11. Is the word "you" confined only to the people present when Jesus said this verse? (question of implication)

12. The coming of the Holy Spirit brought power to the disciples. What kind of power was it? (question of definition)

13. Why must witnessing necessarily begin from Jerusalem? (question of logic)

14. Where is "all Judea"? (question of definition)

15. Where is "Samaria"? (question of definition)

16. There has not been any communication between the Jews and the Samaritans for many years. Why did Jesus mention Samaria in particular? (question of logic)

17. Where is "the ends of the earth"? (question of definition)

18. What are the different ideas, if any, of the concept of "the ends of the earth" for those in Jesus' time and today? On which concept should we base our interpretation? (question of implication)

19. What is Jesus' understanding of "the ends of the earth"? (question of implication)

20. Why did Jesus mention only these four locations? Some of these are

cities and some are regions. Do they have any significance? (question of logic)

21. What is the meaning of "be My witnesses"? (question of definition) What should these witnesses witness? (question of logic)

22. Why did they have to be Jesus' witnesses? (question of logic)

23. Why does one need the power from the Holy Spirit in order to witness? (question of logic)

24. What does the phrase "be My witnesses" reveal about the relationship between Jesus and these witnesses? Do they belong to Jesus? Or are the contents of their witnessing about Jesus? Or are they sent forth by Jesus? (question of relationship)

25. When will these words spoken by Jesus be fulfilled? (question of logic)

26. Jesus was received to Heaven after He said this sentence. What is the significance of understanding this sentence? (question of implication)

27. What is the relationship between this verse and the apostles' ministries afterwards? (question of implication)

Questions remained after sorting and integrating

Why sort and integrate the questions? With too many questions, one may be sidetracked and it may be difficult to focus on the main issues. Some questions are not very important and may not be helpful in interpreting the message of the Scripture. These questions may be eliminated or combined with other questions. After sorting and integrating, we have arrived at the following 15 questions:

1. What is the relationship between this Scripture and its preceding context? Why did Jesus not directly answer the disciples' question, but rather bring out the teaching of this verse?

2. Who is the Holy Spirit? What is His relationship with God the Father and Jesus?

3. When will the Holy Spirit come? What phenomenon occurs when He comes?

4. What is the significance of the Holy Spirit's coming to the disciples at that time?

5. The coming of the Holy Spirit will empower the disciples. What kind of power is it?

6. Why must witnessing begin from Jerusalem?

7. Where are "all Judea" and "Samaria"?

8. There has not been any communication between the Jews and the Samaritans for many years. Why did Jesus mention Samaria in particular?

9. Where is "the ends of the earth"? Where was it in the minds of the disciples then? Where was it in Jesus' mind?

10. Do these four places hold representative significance?

11. What does it mean to be a "witness"? What must be witnessed?

12. Why is it that witnessing needs power from the Holy Spirit?

13. What does the phrase "be My witnesses" reveal about the relationship between Jesus and these witnesses? Do these witnesses belong to Jesus? Are the contents of their witnessing about Jesus? Are the witnesses sent forth by Jesus?

14. Jesus was received to Heaven after He said this sentence. What is the significance of this event?

15. What is the relationship between this verse and the apostles' ministries afterwards?

Step #5: Provide Answers

The following are the answers to the 15 questions on Acts 1:8. They are followed by the interpretation principles employed, listed in brackets:

1. What is the relationship between this Scripture and its preceding context? Why did Jesus not directly answer the disciples' question, but rather bring out the teaching of this verse?

The preceding context quoted the disciples' question to Jesus on the timing of the revival of the kingdom of Israel. All Jews at that time expected that the coming of the promised Messiah would deliver them from all their political enemies. Under the prolonged rule of the Romans, Jewish people had a great anticipation for the Messiah to come and build a kingdom on earth. The question asked by the disciples in 1:6-7 reflected their attitude. *(Contextual study, Historical background)*

First, Jesus pointed out that the timetable for the revival of the kingdom of Israel was not something that they could know (Acts 1:7), and then He changed the subject implying that their question was not the most important one. *(Reasoning with logic)*

The conjunction "But" at the beginning of 1:8 shows that Jesus wanted them to wait for the coming of the Holy Spirit, to be empowered, and to be His witnesses to the ends of the earth. Clearly Jesus was not interested in the building up of a political kingdom on earth, but the expansion of a spiritual one based on His salvation to man established by His death and resurrection. *(Contextual study)*

2. Who is the Holy Spirit? What is His relationship with God the Father and Jesus?

The Holy Spirit is the third person of the Trinity, the triune God. "Trinity" is at the core of evangelical faith. *(Study of words)*

Jesus had promised His disciples that He would send another "advocate" (see John 14:16-17, 16:7-10). *(Analogy of Scriptures)*

"Advocate", or "paraclete" in the original text, is very rich in meaning. Its basic meaning is "calling alongside", and it can have such meanings as "counselor," "mediator," "court witness," "defense lawyer," "deliverer alongside," "personal teacher," etc. *(Study of words)*

"Paraclete" can also be "comrade in battle." In olden days, Greek soldiers fought in teams comprising of two people in each team. Whenever they encountered the enemy, they would stand back to back to maintain a visual range of 360 degrees. The blind spots of one would be covered by the other. *(Historical background)*

He is "another" advocate (John 14:16-17), which implies that He has His own personality, and is not just a power. *(Study of words, Reasoning with logic)*

The Holy Spirit comes to guide the disciples into all truth taught by Jesus (John 16:13). *(Analogy of Scriptures)*

Judging from the second half of Acts 1:8, the Holy Spirit came to grant the disciples heavenly power so that they may be the Lord's witnesses. *(Contextual study)*

Acts chapter 2 described what happened when the Holy Spirit came on the disciples. *(Contextual study)*

3. When will the Holy Spirit come? What phenomenon occurs when He comes?

The phenomenon of the coming of the Holy Spirit was recorded in Acts chapter 2, on the day of Pentecost. The following phenomena were observed: *(Contextual study)*

a. Loud sounds;
b. The blowing of a violent wind;
c. Tongues of fire rested on each of the disciples;
d. They were filled with the Holy Spirit;

e. They spoke in languages they had not learned.

4. What is the significance of the Holy Spirit's coming to the disciples at that time?

From the Scripture, Jesus asked His disciples to wait in Jerusalem for the coming of the Holy Spirit (Acts 1:4), which is equivalent to the "be baptized with the Holy Spirit" (Acts 1:5). The coming of the Holy Spirit is significant to them in the following ways: *(Reasoning with logic)*

a. It fulfilled Jesus' promise to them regarding the Holy Spirit (John 14:16-17, 16:13).
b. It was a continuation of the presence of Jesus with the disciples, and as their advocate, the Holy Spirit guided and helped them accomplish the work that was committed to them.
c. It empowered them so that they would be Jesus' witnesses, which was exceedingly important as they were a fearful group from the time of Jesus' arrest to His death on the cross.

5. The coming of the Holy Spirit will empower the disciples. What kind of power is it?

The power brought forth by the Holy Spirit was not physical power, but spiritual power. This power was related to being a witness for the Lord (see Acts chapters 2 and 4), and it included: *(Contextual study, Analogy of Scriptures)*

a. The ability to speak other countries' languages.
b. The ability to perform miraculous signs.
c. To be filled with courage to witness for the Lord in front of opposing Sanhedrin leaders and antagonistic people.

6. Why must witnessing begin from Jerusalem?

To the disciples at that time, Jerusalem was the center of their religious activities, and the Holy Spirit would also come to them in Jerusalem. It was an entirely natural choice to begin their witnessing from Jerusalem.

As there are three "and" connecting the four places in all three English translation versions, it can be seen that even though their geographic locations go from near to far, witnessing could still take place simultaneously at all places. The conjunction used here was not "then." *(Reasoning with logic)*

7. Where are "all Judea" and "Samaria"?

Looking at the map in Jesus' time, all Judea included the hills of Judea and Judean wilderness, and Jerusalem is located to the north of the hills of Judea.

Samaria was located to the north of all Judea, with major cities including Samaria, Dothan, Tirzah, Shechem, and Shiloh. *(Historical background)*

8. There had not been any communication between the Jews and the Samaritans for many years. Why did Jesus mention Samaria in particular?

John 4:9 says, "For Jews do not associate with Samaritans." The Jews even called them foreigners (or aliens, see translation versions of Luke 17:18), which took place after the Jews returned from Babylon (see the narratives in Ezra and Nehemiah). The Jews did not recognize the Samaritans, regarding them as refugees of captivity by agreeing to intermarry with the Assyrians, thus they were not pure-blooded Israelites. However, the Samaritans vigorously defended the purity of their lineage, and regarded themselves as the true guardians of the law (*Shomerin*).

The returned Jews did not allow the Samaritans to participate in the building of the Holy Temple. Therefore, Samaritans went ahead and built their own temple on Mount Gerizim near Shechem, putting emphasis on the significance of this mountain (see Deut. 27:11-12; John 4:20 "this mountain"). During the Passover festival every year, the Samaritans sacrificed lambs on this mountain as their offerings. The Jews were greatly agitated by such acts, considering it a revulsion against the law's teaching, and treating it as tantamount to idol worship. When the Maccabees ruled Judea (around 130 BC), the Jews had attempted to annihilate the Samaritans.

These historical backgrounds illustrate the huge abyss between the Jews and the Samaritans in Jesus' time. Yet the salvation Jesus accomplished is not just for the Jews, but also for the Samaritans they despised. Therefore, Jesus wanted the Jews to break through the existing barrier and witness to the Samaritans as well, regardless of their standing with other Jews. Clearly the mission is for His Jewish disciples to mend the gap. *(Historical background, Analogy of Scriptures)*

9. Where is "the ends of the earth"? Where was it in the minds of the disciples then? Where was it in Jesus' mind?

In the thinking of the people at that time, "the ends of the earth" refers to where the earth ends. They believed that Rome or Spain in the west were the farthest places on earth, as they thought that the earth is flat and not round. They believed that anyone who sailed westward from Spain would inevitably fall into a deep abyss.

When the Apostle Paul wrote the book of Romans, he expressed a sincere desire to travel to Spain (Romans 15:28), and this probably came from his desire to accomplish the Great Commission. *(Historical background)*

Yet in the mind of Jesus, when He spoke of "the ends of the earth," He was probably referring to places beyond the understanding of people then.

To interpret according to the meaning of this verse, we can say that "the ends of the earth" means "distant places that are inhabited with people." *(Reasoning with logic)*

10. Do these four places hold representative significance?

Evangelization must proceed from near to far, and from small to large. Witnessing must begin locally from Jerusalem, extend to nearby Judea, and include Samaria (which was despised by the Jews), until it reaches every corner of the world.

Taken together, these four places represent the comprehensiveness and generality of witnessing. Jesus Christ wanted His disciples to go wherever there are people to witness the message of His resurrection.

This verse is commonly acknowledged as the key verse in analyzing the structure of the book of Acts. Chapters 1 to 7 are about the disciples witnessing in Jerusalem (see Luke 24:47 "...beginning at Jerusalem"); in chapters 8 and 9 they are witnesses in all Judea and Samaria (see Acts 8:1 "...On that day a great persecution broke out against the church at Jerusalem, and all except the apostles were scattered throughout Judea and Samaria"); and in chapters 10 through 28 they are witnessing "to the ends of the earth." *(Grammatical structure, Analogy of Scriptures, Contextual study)*

11. What does it mean to be a "witness"? What must be witnessed?

The term "witness" here means "the person who witnesses." Simply put, the witness is someone who has actually witnessed certain things happen, had experienced them, and is willing to tell others about what he had experienced. The witness must be faithful to the facts he saw and not confuse facts with speculation. Further, he must not give up the truth for personal gain and be a false witness. *(Study of words)*

Therefore the disciples must not witness only with their mouths, but must also validate the truthfulness of their testimonies by committing their lives. *(Study of words)*

The contents of what was witnessed include the life of Jesus, His deeds, His death, and His resurrection. Through the power of the Holy Spirit the disciple should witness the Word of God and His might. In the many sermons found in the book of Acts, the disciples, headed by Peter, often emphasized these points, the most important being the core of the gospel—the death of Jesus and His resurrection (see 1 Corinthians 15:3-4) —as proof that He is the Messiah promised in the Old Testament. *(Analogy of Scriptures)*

12. Why is it that witnessing needs power from the Holy Spirit?

When the Holy Spirit came on the disciples, they acquired power. The power from the Holy Spirit is the necessary motivation for witnessing. *(Contextual study)*

One will not be convicted of Jesus' salvation through human eloquence or wisdom, but through the work of the Holy Spirit in people's hearts. Jesus Christ said that "He [the Holy Spirit] will convict the world of guilt in regard to sin and righteousness and judgment" (John 16:8). *(Analogy of Scriptures)*

In Acts chapter 2, the hearers felt cut to their hearts and repented after Peter's preaching, and ended up having their lives transformed; these were all works by the Holy Spirit. *(Analogy of Scriptures)*

Jesus knew that to be a faithful witness in a world that opposes God is a daunting task, and He gave the Holy Spirit to be the internal energy source for believers. If a witness lacks this motivating energy source, he is like a car without gas and will not turn on. *(Reasoning with logic)*

13. What does the phrase "be My witnesses" reveal about the relationship between Jesus and these witnesses? Do these witnesses belong to Jesus? Are the contents of their witnessing about Jesus? Are the witnesses sent forth by Jesus?

Grammatically, "My witnesses" mean "witnesses that concern Me," thus the testimony of the witnesses must be about the life of Christ, His death, and His resurrection. *(Grammatical structure)*

14. Jesus was received to the Heaven after He said this sentence. What is the significance of this event?

After Jesus had ascended to heaven, the angels said to the disciples, "Why do you stand here looking into the sky? This same Jesus, who has been taken from you into heaven, will come back in the same way you have seen Him go into heaven." (Acts 1:11) The angels thus reminded the disciples not tarry in this transcendent happening, but to go forward and fulfill the mission given to them until His return. *(Contexual study)*

There are different versions of the Great Commission in the four Gospels (see Matthew 28:19-20; Mark 16:15; Luke 24:47-48; John 20:21). Jesus repeated His command before His ascension (Acts 1:8) to map out a blueprint of the commission, and set boundaries for it, so that the disciples might understand that the scope of the mission is the entire world (Matthew had also mentioned "all nations" in his Gospel). *(Comparative interpretation)*

15. What is the relationship between this verse and the apostles' ministries afterwards?

This verse is commonly acknowledged as the key verse in analyzing the structure of the book of Acts. Chapters 1 to 7 is about the disciples witnessing in Jerusalem (see Luke 24:47 "...beginning at Jerusalem."); chapters 8 and 9 their witnesses in all Judea and Samaria ; and chapters 10 through 28 their witnessing "to the ends of the earth". *(Contextual study, Grammatical structure)*

After the 15 questions are answered, we can validate our conclusions with commentaries. There are 4 commentaries on Acts that will be used as references:

Barrett, C. K. *A Critical and Exegetical Commentary on the Acts of the Apostles.* 2 Volumes. Edinburgh: T & T Clark, 1994.

Bruse, F. F. *The Book of the Acts.* Revised edition. Grand Rapids: Eerdman, 1988.

Longenecker, Richard N. *Acts.* The Expositor's Bible Commentary. Vol. 9. Edited by Frank E. Gaebelein. Grand Rapids: Zondervan, 1981.

Marshall, I. H. *The Acts of the Apostles.* Tyndale New Testament Commentaries 5. Grand Rapids: Eerdman 1980.

Here are 3 commentaries that are readable by most believers, and my insights and their main points are as follows:

1. Commentary by Richard N. Longenecker

This book pointed out two items:

First, Longenecker stressed that this verse is the last command by Jesus before His ascension as well as the main theme of Acts. All the following portion of Acts serves to interpret this verse. It brings out a character, a power and a plan: the character is the Lord Jesus, the power is the Holy Spirit, and the plan is witnessing, from Jerusalem to the ends of the earth.

Second, he quoted the original text to explain that before the two places "all Judea" and "Samaria," there is only one article, indicating that they belong to the same geographical region, but belong to two different nations. This insight is not apparent from reading either the English or the Chinese translations.

2. Commentary by F. F. Bruce

This commentary has only one page ascribed to this verse, yet the author has some notable insights:

Bruce said, "As Jesus had been anointed at his baptism with the Holy Spirit and power, so his followers were now to be similarly anointed and enabled to carry on his work." (p. 36)

In addition, he emphasized that "witness" is a "conspicuous theme" in the book of Acts, and listed the following Scripture to support his view: 2:32, 3:15, 5:32, 10:39, 13:31, 22:15, etc. Further he quoted the two Scriptures Isaiah 43:10 and 44:8, noting that Israel has been called God's witness in the world, but the nation of Israel has not fulfilled this mission, and so Jesus Christ was designated to accomplish this mission.

Bruce also agreed that the geographical places mentioned here (Acts 1:8) is the "content guide" of Acts.

3. Commentary by I. H. Marshall

The author pointed out: "While some have thought that this expression designates Rome, it is much more probable that it has a wider sense; the end of Acts does not mark the completion of the task proposed here, but simply the completion of the first phase." (p. 61)

He also mentioned that these are the last few words uttered by Jesus before His ascension to heaven. Thus it carries particular significance, similar to His last words recorded in Luke (Luke 24:46-49).

Conclusion

In conclusion there are many supplementary views in these commentaries worthy of consulting. Further, from our answers to the 15 questions, there is no major conflict with the conclusions offered by these commentaries. If there is, then we must make careful evaluation to seek a relatively more reasonable answer.

Step # 6: Summarize the Meanings

The meaning of this Scripture can be summarized using three short verbal phrases: the Holy Spirit (will) come, will receive power, and be My witnesses. In addition, this is a commission from the Lord Jesus to His disciples immediately before His ascension.

Step # 7: Find the Controlling Theme

The controlling theme of this Scripture can be written in this way: Jesus commanded His disciples to wait for the Holy Spirit to come on them, and then after they had received power, to be His witnesses in all places, even to the ends of the earth.

Step # 8: Write down the Principle

The step of "Write down the Principle" is to discover spiritual principle that transcend space and time and bridge the historical significance ("controlling theme") of the Scripture to today's readers. If the controlling theme of the Scripture is not processed through this bridging exercise, then it may encounter difficulty in application; and if it is nonetheless applied, then it could bring about dangerous consequences in some cases.

Before we write down this principle, there are several related questions that must be addressed:

1. Must we, as today's believers, still await the coming of the Holy Spirit?

Answer: The Holy Spirit came for all people on the Day of Pentecost; therefore today's believers do not have to "wait" for the coming of the Holy Spirit. At the moment when a believer believes and accepts Christ as his Savior, the Holy Spirit comes to reside in his/her heart immediately. Yet we have to rely on the Holy Spirit, and claim from the indwelling Holy Spirit the power to witness for the Lord.

2. What is the difference between then and now regarding the concept of witnessing to "the ends of the earth"?

Answer: In the minds of the disciples then, witnessing to the ends of the earth may have had a limited scope of geographical areas, which is very different from today's understanding. Yet even if that is the case, if we extend our interpretation of "the ends of the earth" to "distant places inhabited by people", then basically there is no difference.

3. When Jesus commanded His disciples to witness from Jerusalem to the ends of the earth, He was referring to actual geographical areas. How should today's believers apply this command to the strategy and ministry of mission?

Answer: Two paths can be followed in the progressive application of this principle:
- First, treat "Jerusalem" as the city or county in which we live and

consider "all Judea" as nearby counties or states; and then treat "Samaria" as people we may look down on, and then consider taking the gospel to every corner of the world.

- Second, "Jerusalem" can be our relatives; "all Judea" our neighbors, classmates, colleagues, or friends; "Samaria" people we do not quite know or look down on; until we reach everyone on earth.

Taking either of these two paths to evangelize will accomplish the thrust of Jesus' commission: witnessing must begin with local territory. Do not abandon the near in order to approach the far away. And as the four locations are linked together by the conjunction "and" in the Scripture, believers may witness simultaneously in different locations to different groups.

After the above-mentioned "bridging" exercise, we can write down the application principle: "Today's believers must rely on the power given by the Holy Spirit to fulfill a general commission of our Lord, which is to witness to many unto the ends of the earth."

Step # 9: List Specifics

Step #8 has already yielded an application principle: "Today's believers must rely on the power given by the Holy Spirit to fulfill a general commission of our Lord, which is to witness to many unto the ends of the earth."

The following is a tentative specific: "I must rely on the power given by the indwelling Holy Spirit, with my church and my family as the center, preach the gospel to my family, my relatives, my friends, and even people I consider inferior in status."

After writing down the tentative specifics, we should ask, "Is such a specific detailed enough?" On examination, it is clearly not adequate, because it does not name the people to whom the gospel will be preached, when and where it will take place, and how to approach them. Here we list a few detailed applications with sufficient specifics:

1. "I ask for the power of the Holy Spirit in order to witness for the

Lord among my relatives and friends. I am writing down the names of three relatives and friends, and then I will plan out how to begin."

(While leading Bible study, you can ask related questions: "Do you have the power of the Holy Spirit in you to witness?" "Are you willing to pick three persons among your relatives and friends and begin to witness to them?" "How will you bring them to the Lord effectively?")

2. "Every Sunday there are newcomers to the church who are not yet believers. I will work together with the visitation department of the church to find out their names and phone numbers and choose someone who has a background similar to mine, spend a month to visit, and become friends with him/her, and preach the gospel to him/her."

(While leading Bible study, you can ask a related question: "There are several newcomers to your church over the last few weeks. How do you plan to lead them to the Lord?")

3. "I will attend at least one short-term mission this year. I will begin to look out for opportunities and think about who I would go with: maybe with the church or with another mission organization. How do I prepare for funding? Do I go by myself or with my spouse, or with other family members?"

(While leading Bible study you can ask a related question: "Are you willing to take part in a short-term mission this year?" "If you are, how will you plan your activity?")

Step # 10: Put into Action

Put the above listed specifics into action according to the established plan. Before you act, pray about these decisions. You may ask one or two good friends to join you in your plan, or ask them to pray for you so that you may fulfill your plan.

Epilogue

Acts 1:8 is only one Scriptural verse, yet it has yielded a rich harvest of interpretations. It may be an unexpected experience to some brothers and sisters, but at the same time it demonstrates the abundance and depth of biblical messages and concepts.

However, some brothers and sisters may ask, "It takes so much time to thoroughly interpret just one verse! What if I have to interpret a passage or an entire chapter of Scripture? What should I do?"

The truth is that Acts 1:8 is a very special verse. It is the key verse of Acts and thus carries particular significance and an abundance of meaning. The reason for selecting this verse to demonstrate the interpretation method is twofold: on the one hand, it is short and easy to deal with, and can quickly (in fact not too quickly) bring out the essence of the method; on the other hand, I want to show that if one carefully studies a very familiar verse, one can dig out messages that are often missed, which is an important discovery indeed.

There are two paths to proceed in order to learn the "Ten-step Bible Study Method". The first path begins with theory. Understand the theoretical principles and operation procedure of the method, and then utilize this method and procedure to study the Scripture. The other path is on-the-job training: begin by practicing the method on a Scriptural passage (like this study of Acts 1:8), and learn the method through practical training.

This is much like learning how to swim. Not only must one learn the principle, but one must jump into the water to experience, to exercise, and realize the essence of swimming. To study the Bible, one must likewise jump wholeheartedly into Bible study to learn, to investigate, and to dig out the precious messages of the Bible.

It is my sincere wish and desire that brothers and sisters will continue to use the "Ten-step Bible Study Method" to study the Scripture personally as well as to lead Bible studies. In this process you will gain familiarity of its operational procedure and become proficient in it. I wish that this tool will be a lifelong companion to you throughout your Bible study career.

꧁ꩰ꧂

Appendix:
Basic References for Bible Study

(Those with *are recommended by the author)

A. Concordances

*Strong, J. *The Exhaustive Concordance of the Bible.* New York: Abingdon Press, 1980.

Young, R. *Analytical Concordance to the Bible.* Grand Rapids: Eerdmans, rep. 1975.

B. Dictionaries and Lexicons

*Brown, Collin, trans. and ed. *The New International Dictionary of New Testament Theology.* 3 Volumes. Grand Rapids: Zondervan, 1975/1979.

*Elwell, Walter A., ed. *Evangelical Dictionary of Theology.* Grand Rapids: Baker, 1987.

C. Bible Introduction

*Archer, Gleason. *A Survey of Old Testament Introduction.* Rev. ed. Chicago: Moody Press, 1974/1985.

*Carson, D. A. & D. Moo. *An Introduction to the New Testament.* Grand Rapids: Zondervan, 2005.

D. Commentaries

1. One-or-two volume sets

*Walton, J. H., V. H. Matthews & M. Chavalas. *The IVP Bible Background Commentary: Old Testament*. Downers Grove: InterVarsity Press, 2000.

*Walvoord, J. & R. Zuck, eds. *The Bible Knowledge Commentary (Old Testament)*. Wheaton: Victor Books, 1985.

*Walvoord, J. & R. Zuck, eds. *The Bible Knowledge Commentary (New Testament)*. Wheaton: Victor Books, 1983.

2. Series

Expositor's Bible Commentary Series. Grand Rapids: Zondervan, c. 1976-1992.

*NIV Applicaation Commentary. Grand Rapids: Zondervan, 1994-.

*The Tyndale New Testament Commentary Series. Grand Rapids: Tyndale Press, 1956-.

*The Tyndale Old Testament Commentary Series. Downers Grove: InterVarsity Press, 1964-.

E. Study Bibles

*Kaiser, W. & D. Garrett, eds. *NIV Archaeology Study Bible*. Grand Rapids: Zondervan, 2006.

Ryrie Study Bible (New American Standard Translation). Chicago: Moody Press, 1976/1978.

Zondervan NIV Study Bible. Grand Rapids: Zondervan, 2002.

F. Bible Software

1. Pay-ware

*Bibleworks 9 (www.bibleworks.com)
Logos 4 (www.logos.com)

2. Freeware

Bible Gateway (www.biblegateway.com)
e-Sword (www.e-sword.net)
Olivetree (www.olivetree.com)

A Brief Introduction of
Sacred Logos Resource Center

Sacred Logos Resource Center is a non-profit organization registered in USA and Hong Kong. Our head office is located in Sunnyvale, California, USA.

I. Our Vision

A. Living in the postmodern age, there is an urgent need for Chinese churches to go back to the Scriptures and make it the foundation of Christian life and ministries.

B. Since the Scriptures is written for life change, there is also a great need to apply the Scriptural principles to Christian life and ministries.

C. Within the smaller Chinese church setting, there is a lack of full time staff to take care of the daily routine of ministry. As a result, there are not enough manpower and resources to train and equip believers toward maturity and service. On the other hand, the full time staff in bigger churches engaged themselves in various administrative and pastoral duties and therefore do not have time to meet such needs as training and equipping.

Sacred Logos Resource Center is established to fulfill the above mentioned needs.

II. Our Mission

Our mission statement can be summarized in the acronym: SAGOS (**S**ound **A**pplication **G**rounded **O**n **S**criptures)

The ministries of SAGOS aim to assist local churches (both in North America, and overseas, especially China) in training and equipping believers to dig deep into the Word of God with the purpose to enhance skills and to change lives.

Our ministries include going to churches and the mission field by leading seminars on Bible study, Teachers Training, Expository Preaching and other Bible and ministry topics. Also, we publish books, CDs and DVDs for educational and nurturing purposes.

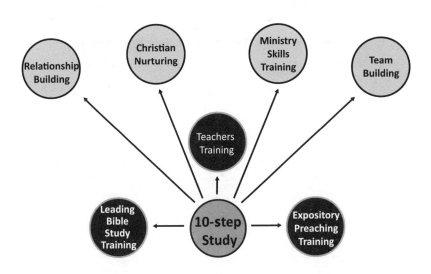

Book Recommendations

Prayer Anthologies (bi-lingual, English and Chinese) complied and translated by Dr. Johann Lai.

The "Ravine" Series — *Prayers of Encouragement*

Echoes from the Ravine — Prayers of Encouragement (volume 1)
Rhymes from the Ravine — Prayers of Encouragement (volume 2)
Whispers from the Ravine — Prayers of Encouragement (volume 3)

The "Ravine" Series contain some effective prayers from Christians through the centuries. These prayers aim to encourage believers not to be deterred by obstacles in life, but dare to take steps to move forward. Therefore, they are useful for meditation and making commitments before the Lord. (*For volume 1, a recitative CD in Chinese Mandarin is attached for listening.*)

The "Whirlwind" Series — *Prayers of Consolation*

Silent Words in the Whirlwind — *Prayers of Consolation (volume 1)*
Heavenly Sounds in the Whirlwind — *Prayers of Consolation (volume 2)*

The "Whirlwind" Series contain prayers of consolation from Christians through the centuries. The theme is taken from the experiences of Job when he was devastated by a "whirlwind" (*Job 1:18-19*), and later God appeared to him in a "whirlwind" to offer comfort (*Job 38:1ff*). The nature of these prayers are for confession, comfort and encouragement, and therefore good for self-reflection and meditation.

The "Throne" Series — *Prayers of Thanksgiving and Praise*

Melodies before the Throne — Prayers of Thanksgiving and Praise (volume 1)
Heartfelt Praises before the Throne — Prayers of Thanksgiving and Praise (volume 2)

The "Throne" Series contain prayers of thanksgiving and praise from Christians through the centuries. They sought to respond to God's manifold blessings and boundless love with sounds of praise in splendid variety.

Introduction of Author

Rev. Johann Lai got his Master of Theology degree (1986) and Doctor of Ministry degree (1991) from Dallas Theological Seminary. He is the founder and President of Sacred Logos Resource Center (SAGOS), and adjunct professor at Christian Witness Theological Seminary (D. Min. program), and Alliance Bible Seminary, Hong Kong (D. Min. program). Rev. Lai has written many books in Chinese, which include *Ten-step Procedure of Bible Study* (1994/2008), *From Stone to Rock — Study on the Life of Peter* (1999), and *Living Faith — An Exposition of James* (2002). He has also compiled a few books of prayers.